INSIDE MLS

NEW YORK RED BULLS

BY KRISTIAN R. DYER

SportsZone

An Imprint of Abdo Publishing
abdobooks.com

abdobooks.com

Published by Abdo Publishing, a division of ABDO, PO Box 398166, Minneapolis, Minnesota 55439.

Printed in the United States of America, North Mankato, Minnesota
052021
092021

THIS BOOK CONTAINS RECYCLED MATERIALS

Cover Photo: Fred Kfoury III/Icon Sportswire/AP Images
Interior Photos: Tim Clayton/Corbis/Corbis Sport/Getty Images, 5, 8–9, 11, 13, 39; David Klein/Cal Sports Media/AP Images, 6; AP Images, 15, 16; Bill Kostroun/AP Images, 18, 21, 23, 25, 36; Al Bello/Allsport/Getty Images Sport/Getty Images, 26; Ezra Shaw/Getty Images Sport/Getty Images, 28; Mel Evans/AP Images, 31; Rich Graessle/Icon Sportswire/AP Images, 33; Doug Pensinger/Getty Images Sport/Getty Images, 35; Steve C. Wilson/AP Images, 40; Nick Wass/AP Images, 42

Editor: Patrick Donnelly
Series Designer: Dan Peluso

Library of Congress Control Number: 2019954385

Publisher's Cataloging-in-Publication Data

Names: Dyer, Kristian R., author.
Title: New York Red Bulls / by Kristian R. Dyer
Description: Minneapolis, Minnesota : Abdo Publishing, 2022 | Series: Inside MLS | Includes online resources and index.
Identifiers: ISBN 9781532192593 (lib. bdg.) | ISBN 9781644945674 (pbk.) | ISBN 9781098210496 (ebook)
Subjects: LCSH: New York Red Bulls (Soccer team)--Juvenile literature. | Soccer teams--Juvenile literature. | New York/New Jersey MetroStars (Soccer team)--Juvenile literature. | Sports Teams--Juvenile literature.
Classification: DDC 796.334--dc23

TABLE OF CONTENTS

CHAPTER 1

FINALLY, A TROPHY

After 18 years, the New York Red Bulls finally had a trophy to celebrate. And the man who led the way also happened to be a legend as both a player and as a head coach.

Mike Petke was named as the head coach of the Red Bulls before the start of the 2013 Major League Soccer (MLS) season. As a player, he was loved by the fans. A native of Long Island, New York, he was drafted in 1998 when the team was called the MetroStars. Petke was all about the team.

The defender was aggressive and gave his all on the field. Family and friends came out to Giants Stadium to support him. He won over fans because he hated to lose. He put in a total effort every time he stepped onto the field. No one cared more about the MetroStars than Petke.

Thierry Henry takes a corner kick for the Red Bulls as they try to wrap up the Supporters' Shield on October 27, 2013.

14
Bulls
Allstate
Bulls

Hans Backe had been a successful coach in Europe, but he couldn't help the Red Bulls win any trophies.

So after a long playing career that ended after the 2010 season, Petke joined the Red Bulls' coaching staff. The head coach at the time was Hans Backe.

Backe was a father figure to the Red Bulls, and with his silver hair, he looked the part too. His experience in Europe as a head coach at several big clubs helped the Red Bulls become one of the best teams in MLS. But in three seasons under Backe, the team never won a trophy.

FIGHTING FOR THE SHIELD

MLS teams compete for three domestic trophies each season. The Supporters' Shield is given to the team that has the best regular-season record. The US Open Cup is an annual knockout tournament open to all professional and amateur teams in the country. And the most coveted prize of all is the MLS Cup. That goes to the winner of the league's postseason playoffs. The champions of the Eastern and Western conferences meet in a one-game, winner-take-all showdown.

In the final game of the 2013 season, the Red Bulls had a chance to win their first trophy. With a win against the Chicago Fire, they could take the Supporters' Shield. Their stadium, Red Bull Arena, was packed, a sold-out crowd excited to see history.

But the fans had a right to be nervous. The team had a long history of falling short in big moments. Even with star players and some very good teams, the Red Bulls had never won a trophy. They had come close, like in 2000, when Petke and his

The Red Bulls' supporters kept the faith despite their team falling behind early.

teammates fell one game short of the MLS Cup. And in 2008, they got hot in the playoffs and made the MLS Cup, only to lose to the Columbus Crew. Would this time be different?

The feeling around the stadium was electric at kickoff, but the opponents weren't intimidated. In the sixth minute, Chicago forward Mike Magee scored to put the visitors up 1–0.

The roaring crowd was suddenly deflated. So much was expected of this team. Would this be another in a long line of disappointments for the club?

After a few moments, though, Red Bull Arena came back to life. The Empire Supporters Club lives by one motto: "As long as we're breathing." That means as long as they are alive, they promise to support the team. This moment was no different. They began to sing and scream, urging on the team. The rest of the stadium began to cheer. The fans would not let the players down, even as they were losing a game that was supposed to change Red Bulls history.

As the minutes ticked by, the supporters kept cheering and jumping up and down. Then in the 24th minute, Thierry Henry rewarded their support.

TYING THE MATCH

A former World Cup winner with France, Henry was the team's captain and its biggest star. The striker had been one of the best players in the world. Now, at age 36, he had to settle for being merely one of the best players in the league. He was still smooth dribbling the ball and—as he would show against Chicago—a fantastic goal scorer.

Henry took a long pass and settled it with his chest. Then from 25 yards out, he placed a perfect shot that rocketed off the crossbar and over the goal line.

Red Bull Arena erupted. Petke, on the sidelines wearing his usual sweater and tie combination, breathed a sigh of relief. It was as if a valve had been opened and all the pressure in the

Team captain Thierry Henry tied the score, and his teammates took care of the rest.

stadium released. Because once the Red Bulls relaxed, the goals came in bunches.

Four more Red Bulls players scored. With each goal, the crowd began to believe more. They believed that they were witnessing history. And they did, with a 5–2 victory for the home team.

The win made it official; the Red Bulls won the Supporters' Shield, capturing the league's best record. It was the first trophy in franchise history.

In postgame celebrations when teams are awarded trophies, the captain is usually the first person to lift the trophy. But Henry refused. He took the Supporters' Shield and walked over to Petke, handing it to the coach.

Henry knew the history. He knew Petke had played on the 1999 MetroStars team, one of the worst teams in the history of MLS. He also knew Petke had played on the 2009 team, which finished with the worst record in the league.

Through all those years and some pretty bad teams, Petke had to have wondered if he and his team

THE EMPIRE SUPPORTERS CLUB

The Empire Supporters Club has backed and followed the MetroStars and then the Red Bulls since their first game. They stand, chant, and sing in unison, waving flags and throwing confetti. They are the oldest supporters' club in MLS, having been formed to root for a different professional team that predated MLS. They're also one of the most respected groups. Their goal is to give the team an emotional lift and be the twelfth player on the field.

An emotional Mike Petke holds the MLS Supporters' Shield after the match.

would ever break through. So when Henry took those long steps over with the Supporters' Shield in his hands, Petke got choked up. Henry insisted Petke be the one to raise the trophy.

"Eighteen years," Henry kept saying as he handed the Supporters' Shield to Petke. "Eighteen years."

After all the suffering and years without a winning team, the Red Bulls were just that—winners. And in his first year as the team's head coach, Petke had won the respect of his players.

With tears in his eyes, Petke raised the trophy. Red Bull Arena erupted. The drought had ended and a legend was born.

CHAPTER 2

SOCCER IN NYC

Today, soccer has become a major sport in the United States. Turn on the television any weekend and games from Mexico, England, Germany, and Spain are easy to find. Big-name European clubs regularly visit the United States in the summer to play exhibition matches. And more people in the United States play soccer than any other sport.

But it wasn't always that way. For most of the 1900s, soccer wasn't very popular in the United States. Then the country hosted the World Cup in 1994, and a spark was lit. That tournament set a record for the best-attended World Cup of all time. Suddenly, soccer looked like it could have a future in the country as a spectator sport.

The legendary Pelé turned New York Cosmos matches into major events when he arrived in 1975.

West Germany's Franz Beckenbauer (6) was one of many international stars who played for the Cosmos.

Of course, the United States needed a professional league to help continue the growth of the sport. The US Soccer Federation agreed to create and support a top-level pro league when it was granted the rights to the 1994 World Cup. And two years after that tournament, MLS was born.

The New York/New Jersey MetroStars were among the original 10 teams that first season. They played their games in

Giants Stadium in East Rutherford, New Jersey. Just minutes away from the stadium stood the New York City skyline. Tall skyscrapers and majestic bridges reminded fans and players that they were playing in the biggest metropolitan area in the country.

That meant something, because in the 1970s, the New York Cosmos also called Giants Stadium home. The Cosmos played in the North American Soccer League (NASL), the most successful of a handful of attempts at professional soccer in the United States.

Major international players such as Franz Beckenbauer of West Germany, Giorgio Chinaglia of Italy, and Carlos Alberto of Brazil finished out their careers playing for the Cosmos. But no player attracted fans quite like Brazilian maestro Pelé, who played for the Cosmos from 1975 to 1977. The NASL eventually folded, but the legacy of that star-studded team remained. It was this legacy that the MetroStars inherited.

The early years of the team were difficult. Despite boasting big-name players such as Italian national team midfielder Roberto Donadoni and US World Cup stars such as Tab Ramos and Tony Meola, the MetroStars had difficulties. They missed the playoffs twice in the league's first four years. That was

MetroStars goalkeeper Tony Meola, *left*, talks with the team's first head coach, Eddie Firmani, on the grass field at Giants Stadium in April 1996.

hard to take for fans who had been used to the success of the Cosmos, who won five NASL titles in 11 years with their world-class players.

The 2000 season was different. One year earlier, the MetroStars had finished 7–25, the worst record in the league.

They brought in a new coach, Octavio Zambrano, who'd had success in MLS with the Los Angeles Galaxy. Another key addition was Nick Sakiewicz, hired to be the general manager. Sakiewicz had recently put together a successful team with the Tampa Bay Mutiny. Born and raised in New Jersey, he accepted the challenge of overhauling a team that had failed miserably in 1999.

International players such as Colombian national team forward Adolfo Valencia helped the attack. Trades within MLS added a number of impact players, including defenders Steve Jolley and Daniel Hernández. But in the biggest trade, Sakiewicz acquired young American forward Clint Mathis from the Galaxy.

Mathis became a star in New York. His dynamic offensive game not only helped the MetroStars. It helped him land a spot on the US national team.

The MetroStars' turnaround in 2000 included a 17–12–3 record and a first-place finish in the Eastern Conference. Though they lost to the Chicago Fire in the league semifinals, the season appeared to be a step in the right direction.

Instead, the MetroStars failed to build off that momentum. The team wouldn't finish higher than fifth in the league for the rest of the decade.

BECOMING THE RED BULLS

In the midst of those mediocre seasons, the club made a big change. Just weeks before the start of the 2006 season, the MetroStars were sold to the Red Bull energy drink corporation. Based in Austria, the company already owned a team in that country and had other sporting interests. They bought the MetroStars, renamed them the New York Red Bulls, and sought to change the team's look and way of doing business.

Some fans were upset about the change. They saw the new name as an insult and didn't want to cheer for a team named after an energy drink. To this day, many fans of the team still lovingly refer to the team as 'Metro' and refuse to acknowledge the name change. It isn't uncommon to still see MetroStars jerseys at games.

The first few years under new ownership weren't smooth ones. The team hired former US national team coach Bruce Arena during the 2006 season. One year later, he was joined by New Jersey native and former US national team star Claudio Reyna and Colombian forward Juan Pablo Ángel. Even so, the

The team changed its name and uniforms to reflect new ownership, but the Red Bulls weren't much more successful than the MetroStars at first.

team wasn't much better than the MetroStars squads of years past. But Red Bull the company was learning and growing. It was new to MLS and American sports. It would take time.

STEPPING UP

The 2010 season proved to be a big one for the club. That year, the team moved into a brand new, state-of-the-art stadium. It also signed French striker Thierry Henry, a world-class goal scorer. Henry would be a success in New York, scoring 51 goals and being named to the league's Best XI three times.

Other stars such as Australian midfielder Tim Cahill joined him, raising the talent level of the team. Still, it took until 2013 for the Red Bulls to win a trophy, when they captured their first Supporters' Shield. But players such as Henry lifted the organization from being a joke to commanding a certain level of respect.

After Henry retired in 2014, the Red Bulls went in a different direction. They stopped signing star players to big contracts. Instead, they focused on developing young players through their academy. With the stars gone, many assumed the Red Bulls would struggle to

RED BULL ARENA

As MLS grew, the league encouraged teams to build their own soccer-specific stadiums. In 2010 the Red Bulls opened one of the league's best. Red Bull Arena is in Harrison, New Jersey, not far from New York City. The 25,000-seat stadium features a gorgeous grass field that is the envy of the rest of MLS. The seats are covered by a roof, allowing fans to sit in comfort no matter the weather.

Fans head to see the first official game at Red Bull Arena on March 27, 2010.

maintain their lofty standards. Instead, a team that frequently was among the youngest in the league would find new success.

Through 2020 the Red Bulls hadn't won an MLS Cup, but they added Supporters' Shields to their trophy case in 2015 and 2018. Young players such as Matt Miazga, Tyler Adams, and Sean Davis became stars for the Red Bulls, leading to a new and exciting direction for the franchise.

CHAPTER 3

SUPER STARS AND BULLS

As the MetroStars and then the Red Bulls, New York has always had star players. The first player to sign with an MLS team was Tab Ramos with the MetroStars. Ramos was a joy to watch on the field. The US World Cup veteran was a creative midfielder who loved to dribble the ball and attack. For Ramos, having grown up in New Jersey near Giants Stadium, it was a dream to play for the MetroStars.

Ramos wasn't the only star of those early MetroStars teams. Roberto Donadoni, who played for Italy in the 1994 World Cup, was one of the few big-name international players in MLS. Over two seasons with the MetroStars, he proved to be a hard worker and a good passer. Donadoni also

Tab Ramos acknowledges fans before his final regular-season home game for the MetroStars on September 12, 2002.

10

Clint Mathis brought his goal-scoring talents to New York in 2000.

served as a veteran role model for the younger players on the MetroStars.

Tony Meola played goalkeeper for the United States in two World Cups. Like Ramos, he grew up in New Jersey. Meola was a fan favorite and brought star power to the MetroStars as one of the best goalkeepers in MLS.

YOUNG AMERICAN STARS

As the league grew, so did the MetroStars' ability to find young players. And the MetroStars developed a number of young American stars who would go on to play for big teams in Europe and even star in the World Cup.

In 2000 the MetroStars acquired Clint Mathis from the LA Galaxy. The young forward blossomed in New York and became a star for the US national team at the 2002 World Cup. Mathis scored a crucial goal for the United States in a 1–1 tie with South Korea. The Americans shocked the world in the tournament, advancing to the quarterfinals. Mathis later played professionally in Germany and Greece.

At the same time that Mathis was emerging, goalkeeper Tim Howard was bursting onto the stage in MLS. Born in central New Jersey, Howard was a standout in soccer and basketball in high school.

He signed with the MetroStars right after high school in 1998 and quickly impressed. He had good reflexes and played with maturity. He became the team's starting goalkeeper in 2001. Before long some of the biggest clubs in the world started to notice him. In 2003 Howard moved to English Premier League powerhouse Manchester United. Howard went on to an accomplished career in England and represented the United States at three World Cups.

Several years later, two more up-and-coming Americans showed up. Midfielder Michael Bradley played with the MetroStars in 2005. Forward Jozy Altidore was there from 2006 to 2008. Both left for Europe and later returned to MLS as established stars with Toronto FC. Each played key roles for the US national team. And both got their professional starts in New Jersey.

THE RED BULL ERA

When Red Bull bought the team in 2006, the company began to spend money on big-name players. That became especially true in 2007, when the league changed its rules. Teams could now have "designated players," or highly paid players who didn't count against the otherwise low salary cap. The Red Bulls brought in forward Juan Pablo Ángel using this rule in 2007, and he lived up to the billing.

The forward arrived from Aston Villa in England in 2007 and went on to become one of the best players in Red Bulls history.

Tim Howard, *left*, makes a save for the MetroStars in 2003.

Ángel scored 58 goals over the next four years with the Red Bulls. He was also a star for the Colombian national team.

In 2010 the Red Bulls got even more aggressive. Thierry Henry had proven to be one of the world's best goal-scorers. He had won a World Cup while playing for France and starred for major clubs Arsenal and Barcelona. Following the arrival of David Beckham to the Galaxy in 2007, Henry became the second global superstar to join MLS.

Henry seemed to be able to score from anywhere on the field. The relentless attacker helped change the perception of the Red Bulls. He instantly made the Red Bulls one of the top teams in MLS. In 2020, Henry returned to MLS as coach of the Montreal Impact.

Before he signed with the Red Bulls in 2013, striker Bradley Wright-Phillips thought about retiring. He wasn't playing very much in his native England and was frustrated. But after a successful tryout with the Red Bulls, he found a good fit in New York. Over seven seasons, the humble Wright-Phillips twice led the league in scoring. When the club parted ways with him after the 2019 season, Wright-Phillips left with a team-record 126 goals across all competitions.

Thierry Henry, *left*, and Seth Stammler celebrate a Red Bulls goal in 2010.

"Brad will go down as one of the best forwards in MLS history," Red Bulls sporting director Denis Hamlett said.

A NEW MOVEMENT

When the Red Bulls hired Jesse Marsch as their head coach in 2015, a new era began for the team. Smart and energetic,

Bradley Wright-Phillips heads the ball toward the goal in a 2019 match.

Marsch helped transform the roster from one filled with aging Europeans to a team of young players with their futures still ahead of them. His teams ran hard and were aggressive. After three and a half seasons, Marsch left to coach for Red Bull's team in Salzburg, Austria.

One of Marsch's young players, defender Matt Miazga, grew up playing in the Red Bulls Academy. Despite turning 20 during the 2015 season, he started at central defender on the team that won the Supporters' Shield that year. Shortly thereafter Miazga left to continue his career in Europe.

Marsch played a big role in turning midfielder Tyler Adams into a star. Signed by the Red Bulls as a teenager, Adams was a local player from New York's Hudson Valley who grew up playing for the team's academy. He developed into a regular with the MLS team and by age 19 was already playing for the US national team. Sensing his bright future, the Red Bulls' sister team, RB Leipzig in Germany, acquired Adams following the 2018 season.

THE TOP 25

To celebrate its 25th season, in 2020 MLS named its 25 best players of all time. Red Bulls/MetroStars legends Bradley Wright-Phillips and Tony Meola were among those named to the team. Five others who spent time with the organization made the cut. They were Jeff Agoos, Dwayne De Rosario, Kevin Hartman, Jaime Moreno, and Eddie Pope.

Not all was lost, though. RB Leipzig had to pay for Adams. That money could then go back into the academy, where the team could try to unearth more talented players. Meanwhile, the club looked to other talented players such as defender Aaron Long and midfielders Caden Clark and Kaku to continue leading the first team into the future.

CHAPTER 4

NEW YORK MINUTES

Giants Stadium, home of the MetroStars, was one of the host stadiums for the 1994 World Cup. Every match there was played before a sellout crowd. That soccer fever carried over to 1996, when the MetroStars drew more than 46,000 fans for their first match on April 20. That wasn't a sellout in the huge American football stadium. But it was an impressive showing for a brand-new league.

The weather was amazing for that time of year, and the game itself was memorable, too. Just not in the way MetroStars fans wanted it to be. With the MetroStars and New England Revolution scoreless and just seconds left to play, MetroStars defender Nicola Caricola kicked a simple cross into his own goal, giving the Revolution a 1–0 win.

Defender Nicola Caricola made an infamous miscue in the MetroStars' first home match.

METROSTARS
5

Steve Jolley jumps onto the pile as the MetroStars celebrate an overtime victory against Dallas in the 2000 MLS playoffs.

Caricola was supposed to be a star player for the MetroStars, and his mistake was embarrassing. That moment became known as "the Curse of Caricola," because it supposedly set the team up for years of bad luck. Any time something went wrong for the MetroStars, fans would look back at this moment as a bad omen for the franchise.

WINNING WAYS

While the team wouldn't win a trophy until 2013, the early years still had their share of highlights. One of the most exciting MetroStars seasons came early in their existence.

After a 7–25 finish in 1999, the MetroStars hired Nick Sakiewicz to be their new general manager. He in turn hired a great coach in Octavio Zambrano. Sakiewicz then signed several key international players and brought in defender Steve Jolley and forward Clint Mathis.

The team didn't win an MLS Cup under Sakiewicz, but the 2000 season was one of the best the franchise has ever seen. For the first time since MLS started in 1996, the MetroStars were one of the best teams in the league. They scored lots of goals and were fun to watch. They had young players and rising stars. Fans who had grown tired of the losses began returning to Giants Stadium excited by the MetroStars.

The MetroStars finished with the third-best record in the league. Then they defeated Dallas in the league quarterfinals before losing to Chicago in the semifinals. Some observers say that the 2000 MetroStars are among the best teams in league history to not win the MLS Cup.

THE SHIELD

In 2018 the Red Bulls clinched their third Supporters' Shield at home at Red Bull Arena on the last day of the regular season. The actual trophy wasn't in New Jersey, however. It was in Canada, where first-place Atlanta United was expected to win its game against Toronto the same day. But Atlanta lost and the Red Bulls leap-frogged into first with a victory. Without a trophy, the Red Bulls had no prize for the celebration. But one fan went to the Halloween weekend game dressed as superhero Captain America. He offered his homemade shield to the players, who used it to celebrate the win.

RUN TO THE CUP

MLS was changing in the mid-2000s. Some believed the league was going to fold early in the decade. However, changes began bringing new life to the league. One of those changes was happening in New York.

The team took on the Red Bulls name in 2006. Soon it was taking advantage of new rules to sign high-priced star players. And in the 2008 playoffs, the team from the United States' biggest city finally looked like a contender.

It wasn't an easy season. The team sold the contract of its young star forward, Jozy Altidore, to a European club that summer. Other key players were injured

The Red Bulls celebrate their surprise 2018 Supporters' Shield victory with a makeshift Captain America shield.

or suspended. But behind new coach Juan Carlos Osorio and 14 goals from Juan Pablo Ángel, New York sneaked into the playoffs as the last wild card. Under the playoff format of the time, New York was placed into the Western Conference bracket. And the Red Bulls soon began rolling.

Red Bulls head coach Juan Carlos Osorio, *right*, hugs forward Juan Pablo Ángel after New York clinched a trip to the 2008 MLS Cup with a 1–0 win over Real Salt Lake.

New York upset the defending champion, Houston Dynamo, in the first round. Ángel scored in each game. The Red Bulls won 4–1 on aggregate. They then went to Real Salt Lake for the winner-take-all conference final. Playing in Salt Lake's new stadium, Dave van den Bergh put New York up in the 28th minute. Then the Red Bulls had to hold on. It was a tight game. Salt Lake pressed and pressed. Despite some close chances, Real Salt Lake couldn't find the back of the net. New York won 1–0 to advance to its first MLS Cup.

The dream run ended in Carson, California. Playing the Supporters' Shield–winning Columbus Crew, the Red Bulls fell 3–1. After 13 years of disappointment, though, the team had shown it could contend with the very best.

"I'm really proud of what we achieved this year, after all the problems and all the new players," Ángel said. "It doesn't mean I'm happy that we lost, but we lost to the best team."

WRIGHT-PHILLIPS HITS THE CENTURY MARK

Bradley Wright-Phillips scored 108 goals in six seasons with the Red Bulls. He led the team in scoring five straight seasons. His 27 goals in 2014, his first year in New York, led the league and established a team record. He also led MLS with 24 goals in 2016. But Red Bulls fans will always remember his 100th and the celebration that followed.

Wright-Phillips models his special jersey after scoring his 100th career MLS goal.

Wright-Phillips made history on July 25, 2018. The Red Bulls' talented striker, who wore jersey No. 99, entered the game with 99 career MLS goals. It didn't take him long to score his milestone goal against DC United.

In the game's second minute, Wright-Phillips split two United defenders to run down a long pass from midfield. After gathering the ball in the penalty area, Wright-Phillips sent a low shot between the legs of a defender. The ball skipped under diving goalkeeper David Ousted and into the net for his 100th MLS goal.

Before his teammates could mob him, Wright-Phillips unveiled his own special celebration. He tore off his No. 99 jersey to reveal a second jersey, this one with the No. 100 on the back. He was the 11th player in MLS history to score 100 goals, and he did it in 159 games. That broke the record for fewest games to reach the 100-goal mark, previously held by Taylor Twellman with 174.

LUIS ROBLES

Luis Robles first took the field for the Red Bulls in 2012. Over the next eight seasons, the Arizona native played 238 league games for the team. At one point he started an MLS-record 183 in a row. During his time with New York, Robles also helped the team win the Supporters' Shield and was named MLS Goalkeeper of the Year in 2015. However, the team did not re-sign Robles after the 2019 season, and the former captain joined Inter Miami.

Wright-Phillips moved on to Los Angeles FC after scoring twice in 24 games for New York in 2019. He helped the Red Bulls qualify for the playoffs in his final season, but they lost a first-round knockout match to the Philadelphia Union.

TIMELINE

1995
US national team midfielder Tab Ramos becomes the first player signed by MLS and is assigned to the MetroStars.

1996
The MetroStars lose their first game against the LA Galaxy before a big crowd at the Rose Bowl. One week later, they lose 1–0 at home to the New England Revolution.

2000
The team wins the Eastern Conference with a young squad that includes several star international players.

2006
The Red Bull energy drink corporation buys the MetroStars and renames the team the New York Red Bulls.

2008
The Red Bulls make it to their first MLS Cup, but the Columbus Crew defeat them 3-1.

2010
The team moves to Red Bull Arena in Harrison, New Jersey, and signs star attacker Thierry Henry.

2013
The Red Bulls, under first-year coach Mike Petke, win the first trophy in franchise history when they capture the Supporters' Shield.

2015
The Red Bulls win the Supporters' Shield in their first season under coach Jesse Marsch.

2018
Midfielder Tyler Adams becomes the first New York player to move to sister club RB Leipzig in Germany.

2018
The Red Bulls win yet another Supporters' Shield while setting an MLS record for most points in a season under coach Chris Armas.

TEAM FACTS

FIRST SEASON

1996

STADIUMS

Giants Stadium (1996–2009)
Red Bull Arena (2010–)

SUPPORTERS' SHIELDS

2013, 2015, 2018

KEY PLAYERS

Tyler Adams (2016–18)
Juan Pablo Ángel (2007–10)
Amado Guevara (2003–06)
Thierry Henry (2010–14)
Clint Mathis (2000–03, 2007)
Tony Meola (1996–98, 2005–06)
Tab Ramos (1996–2002)
Luis Robles (2012–19)
Bradley Wright-Phillips (2013–19)

KEY COACHES

Chris Armas (2018–20)
Hans Backe (2010–12)
Bob Bradley (2003–05)
Jesse Marsch (2015–18)
Mike Petke (2013–14)
Octavio Zambrano (2000–02)

MLS MOST VALUABLE PLAYER

Amado Guevara (2004)

MLS DEFENDER OF THE YEAR

Aaron Long (2018)

MLS GOALKEEPER OF THE YEAR

Tim Howard (2001)
Luis Robles (2015)

MLS HUMANITARIAN OF THE YEAR

Tim Howard (2001)
Steve Jolley (2002)
Seth Stammler (2010)

MLS ROOKIE OF THE YEAR

Rodrigo Faria (2001)

MLS COACH OF THE YEAR

Jesse Marsch (2015)

GLOSSARY

academy
A series of youth teams run by a professional club where young players can train to one day become professional soccer players.

aggregate
The combined score of two games in a playoff series.

defender
A player whose job is to keep the other team from taking shots and scoring.

forward
A player whose job is to score goals.

general manager
An executive who runs a team and is responsible for finding and signing players.

goalkeeper
A player whose primary duty is to prevent the ball from entering the net.

international
A label often applied to players who represent their national team.

midfielders
The players who link the defenders with the offensive attack.

supporters' club
A group of fans who stand and cheer loudly to support their team.

Supporters' Shield
A trophy given to the MLS team with the best regular-season record.

MORE INFORMATION

BOOKS

Kortemeier, Todd. *Total Soccer*. Minneapolis, MN: Abdo Publishing, 2017.

Marthaler, Jon. *Ultimate Soccer Road Trip*. Minneapolis, MN: Abdo Publishing, 2019.

Trusdell, Brian. *Soccer Record Breakers*. Minneapolis, MN: Abdo Publishing, 2016.

ONLINE RESOURCES

Booklinks
NONFICTION NETWORK
FREE! ONLINE NONFICTION RESOURCES

To learn more about the New York Red Bulls, please visit **abdobooklinks.com** or scan this QR code. These links are routinely monitored and updated to provide the most current information available.

INDEX

ABOUT THE AUTHOR

Kristian R. Dyer has covered MLS since 2005 for outlets such as ESPN.com and The Athletic. In addition, he is a regular on the Red Bulls pregame broadcast on MSG Network. He played college soccer at Montclair State University. He lives in New Jersey with his wife and their son.